THE EIFFEL TOWER

Winnie Denker Françoise Sagan

Text Françoise Sagan
Photographs and captions Winnie Denker
Design Sheldon Cotler

THE EIFFEL TOWER

Winnie Denker Françoise Sagan

The Eiffel Tower
has watched over Paris for a hundred years
and to celebrate this centenary
it has been clothed in new lighting.
Winnie Denker has scoured the streets and
rooftops of Paris
to capture the Sentry of Paris
in all its various moods.

ANDRE DEUTSCH

1900 L'EXPOSITION N 128 — J

FIGARO ILLUSTRÉ

Cliché Neurdein frères. VUE PANORAMIQUE DE LA TOUR EIFFEL ET DU GLOBE CÉLESTE, PRISE DE LA SEINE Typogravure Goupil, Paris.

ÉDITEURS

MANZI, JOYANT & Cie | LE FIGARO

24, boulevard des Capucines | *26, rue Drouot*

PARIS

Prix : 3 fr. ; l'étranger : 3 fr. 50

I went to have a look at the exhibition; I had been commissioned to write an article. But I was lost for words: the Eiffel tower surpassed my wildest dreams.

Stéphane Mallarmé.

Poised ready to spar, head high, body tensed up, a thousand ecstatic cosmopolitan ants swarming constantly up and down it, the Eiffel Tower today seems touchingly invulnerable to us Parisians. And yet . . . and yet . . . it only narrowly escaped demolition; twice. The first time shortly after building work began, and again twenty years after its christening. But can one now even imagine a sinister, featureless Champ de Mars, with tourists feeling unaccountably frustrated, a Paris seen from the air and yet indistinguishable from any other capital city?

They had barely begun work on the Tower when a petition was got up, signed by all the leading lights of the time, including Leconte de Lisle, Guy de Maupassant, Dumas fils, Sardou, Gounod, François Coppée, Sully Prudhomme and Verlaine, a respectable petition, ergo, demanding that the "metal monstrosity" be scrapped forthwith. This outraged elite invoked, among other things, the noble past of Lutetia, the Kings of France, History, etc. . . . Now it is precisely when History and Respect get thrown into the arena with Aesthetics that trouble ensues. One need only recall the public outcry about the famous pyramid recently built in front of the Louvre and deemed

We the undersigned writers, painters, sculptors, architects, passionate devotees of Paris's beauty, intact until now, have come to protest with all the power and vehemence at our command, in the face of faltering French good taste, and of the threat now posed to the very art and history of France, against the construction of the useless and monstrous Eiffel Tower at the heart of our city, which the public, habitually the benchmark of good sense and fairness, has already mischievously christened the Tower of Babel.

so disfiguring. The Louvre, that is, which had been given a facelift by Haussmann's architect one hundred and fifty years before, after he had designed the Au Printemps department store and before starting work on the ring road! . . . Need I say more. Having called on History, they mobilized Aesthetics. The fashion, "La Mode", was predominantly pastoral, full of fussy detail, delicate niceties, affectations, all of which threw up their tiny hands in horror at the brutality, clean lines and modernity of the Tower. It was variously described as a Cyclops, a grating, a suppository, an edifice, a pillar, obelisk, skeleton, lamppost, watch-tower etc. . . . each term masculine and qualified by one of the more unpleasant adjectives. This lasted some time, and even Eiffel got worried; until some unknown Parisian, a bit more daring, cynical or short-sighted than the others decreed the Tower to be female. Everything suddenly fell into place. With the change in gender, the lack of usefulness, the precariousness, the grace and fragility all became explicable. Only Aragon could have made this sort of comment on the sleight of hand: "But the very best moment was when the Eiffel Tower let us glimpse utterly unexpected female genitalia between her open iron legs."

At a stroke the Tower became a giraffe, a shepherdess, a guitar, an aviary, . . . all feminine names and combined with the most charming epithets. And here we

Letter of February 1887 addressed to M. Alphand, construction director for the 1889 exhibition. It was signed by Charles Gounod, Charles Garnier, Victorien Sardou, Eugène Guillaume, Alexandre Dumas, François Coppée, Leconte de Lisle, Daumais, Sully Prudhomme, Guy de Maupassant . . .

remain: thus can Irwin Shaw, like a good logical American, be amazed at "the strange logic of the French language which will class such an enormous phallic symbol as feminine." And so now, in practice, no one would dream of describing the Tower in masculine terms. The Arc de Triomphe certainly, and the Sacré Cœur and the Invalides; but SHE, the Tower, protects the rather confused macho French who will, curiously, only tolerate being protected by a woman, be she Jeanne d'Arc or Jeanne Hachette; who even sent that young country, America, a decidedly fleshy statue of Liberty.

This may all be no more than a series of coincidences; perhaps my hypothesis is false . . . and, in any case, since Aragon is no longer around to support me, I will retract it willingly. Even so it is charming to think that to please Parisians, they had to make the Eiffel Tower feminine.

Let us turn our attention to the tiresome and corpulent body of fact. The *Exposition Universelle* of 1889 promised to be among the best in the world. People were to see displayed Nature and all her works, and man and all his. Trees and houses, plants and artifacts, minerals and jewels, animals and furs, herbs and hookahs, chalks and boards; every kind of shelter man had made from the storm, every type of cloth the changing seasons had required; every medicine needed to combat the ravages of time. And on top of that, people were to find all the objects, the improbable devices, the ingenious discoveries which, having started life as lumps of ore under the ground or as fibres enmeshed in a plant, had ended up satisfying the appetite of distance and being transformed into vertiginous contraptions called train, vehicle, machine. All the various countries would be lining up not only to say "Look what I've got", but also this time to say "Look what I've done with mine", a different exciting challenge. And Paris, Paris the Ville Lumière, queen of cities, the capital of capitals, Paris had to be, had to have the star attraction. But what? It had to be visible to all, it had to be unmistakeable, unique, new and incredible. After some weeks of thought the Official Newspaper published the rules of a competition "open to French architects and engineers" asking them to study the possibility of building an iron tower on the

La tour grandit et, sur son faîte,
Invincible, dressant la tête,
L'Homme, ouvrant tout grands ses yeux
/clairs,
Pourra, dans ses jeux ordinaires,
Prendre dans ses mains les tonnerres,
Et jouer avec les éclairs.
Théodore de Banville.

The Nicaragua Pavilion and the Portugal Pavilion at the river's edge

Walking beneath the exhibition's star attraction

Champ de Mars, on a square base of 125 metres each side, and 300 metres high. They were to make a model of this tower on a plan of the Champ de Mars, and if they saw fit, to present an alternative plan without the said tower.

Clearly, the tower in itself was already far-fetched enough at this stage that suggestions for alternatives or replacements were needed. And of course, 300 metres was ludicrous! It was actually completely insane, because the two tallest buildings in the world were the Washington obelisk and the Turin tower, neither of which exceeded 169 metres. So, something 300 metres high on a base of 125 metres was unbelievable, it was just too much! Yes, 300 metres was too tall, but then again it would be precisely tall enough to stun the whole world, which was exactly what was required. One hundred and seven entries were submitted, only Eiffel's design was considered, and the foundations were laid in January 1887.

To begin with, Parisians bestowed the same sort of sympathy on the project that they might normally have reserved for a child they knew would never be born, or who would die at birth. And as for the Tower's immediate neighbours in the apartment blocks overlooking the Champ de Mars, they became quite hysterical, demanding to be insured against it. As the city of Paris was asking for a year's grace to investigate possibilities and to sort out the paperwork, even though it was a sleeping partner in the venture, Eiffel insured the neighbours personally! He was already covering two-thirds of the costs himself – with the proviso that he be sole beneficiary of the Tower for the first twenty years. He must have been terribly sure of himself . . .

And rightly so! The legs went up, a bit ridiculous, then the floor of the first level, making it look like an enormous raised pie; then they launched into the second stage, culminating in the second-storey platform, and swiftly on to the third stage: to general amazement! The builders worked all day and in all weathers, in the summer heat and the gales of winter. (And this was a time when winter was wintry and summer

NICARAGUA

WATER CLOSETS

These engineer architects have created a new decorative art, which utilizes ornamental bolts, iron quoins edging the grand line, a sort of gothic lace in iron. We rediscover something of this in the Eiffel Tower.

Paul Gauguin

summery.) It was a strange thing and a rare thing, but there were no accidents: not one man fell from this dizzying Tower. And there were one hundred and fifty builders, sometimes nearer two hundred, of whom only a certain number were skilled "Compagnons". But safety was paramount on Eiffel's site, in contrast with the enormous bridge being built at the same time in Scotland

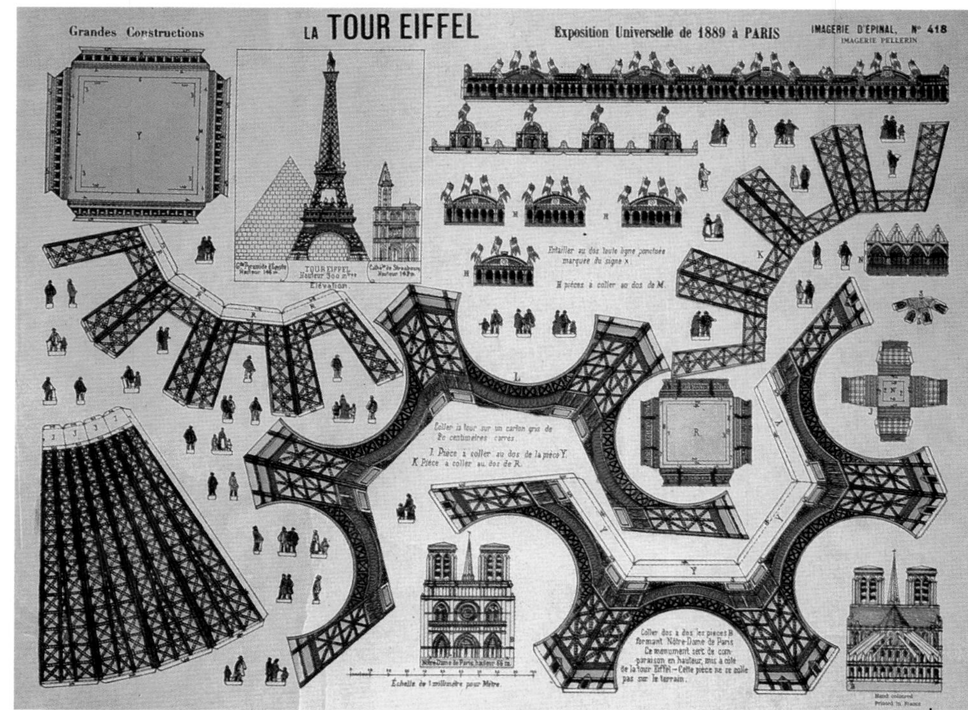

But all the same his Tower looked like a factory chimney under construction, or like a skeleton waiting to be filled by freestone or bricks. It was impossible to conceive that this funnel-shaped criss-cross of lattices was finished, that this solitary and pitted suppository would remain at it was.
Joris Karl Huysmans

which claimed more than one hundred lives in five years. And Eiffel had only one strike in the two years, at a time when life was hard and workers desperate enough to risk confrontations.

During the course of construction there had first been the petition, then the turnaround in public opinion, but from the outset there had also been the tourists who would just stand there at the bottom, necks craned, gawping in amazement. Already. And on March 31 1889 the Tower was duly completed, and some important personages came with Eiffel and his builders to christen it. As, naturally enough, the lifts were not working, the column of besuited and behatted gents stepped boldly forward up the stairs. Alas, alack! as they say: with the exception of Eiffel, who was accustomed to the climb and propelled himself indefatigably upwards with easy swinging gait, the little crowd became so many disparate stragglers. One deputy felt peculiar upon arrival at the first level, but continued his ascent blindfolded, while others staggered about the platform panting and gasping. The sight-seers down below, held in check by the gendarmes, collapsed with mirth – of the fifty guests only twenty reached the top of the 1710 steps, and they were in no kind of shape! With tears, of emotion, in his eyes, Eiffel himself hoisted the seven-and-a-half by four-and-a-half-metre

flag, a gift from his workers. A twenty-one gun salute was fired. Here was the first ever flag to fly on a mast 300 metres high. And that is why, on his descent, Eiffel received the Légion d'honneur.

The following month saw the battle for the lifts: Otis, without Pifre, built the north and south pillar lifts; Edoux, minus Samain, did the second stage and Roux-Combaluzier, in partnership with a certain Lepape, took charge of the rest. It was one of the great lift races of all time! . . . even if, on the day of the great jamboree, Tuesday May 7 1889, when the floodgates were opened amidst Bengal lights, republican guards and rifle fire, they were still not working. There was a fine turnout for this solemn inauguration! There was Abdker, son of Khédive, His Majesty the King of Siam, His Majesty Ranavalo the sovereign of Madagascar, the Bey of

I bring to the tower the testimony of a tireless pilgrim from the four corners of the world. In the towns, the savannah, the pampas, in the desert, on the Gaths and on the estuaries – everywhere – and among the downtrodden as well as the rest, the tower is a symbol of beloved Paris, and a beloved symbol of Paris in everybody's heart.

Le Corbusier

Family pictures. From left to right: *Eiffel with his grandson; with his son-in-law and collaborator, M. Solles, at the top of the tower; with his daughter. Artist's impression of Gustave Eiffel*

Djibouti Nasser ed Din, the Shah of Persia, the Lord Mayor of London, the Princess of Wagram, Alexander of Serbia, President Carnot, Marie-Christine of Spain and many others. All the ministers, all the princes, all the artists, shopgirls, and crowds of Paris. And Eiffel wrote in the visitors' book-cum-log, "Exhibition open, entry of public, at last! Signed: Eiffel". The show was open. And France held the key: without the shadow of a doubt! Because the whole world was enthralled with this young giantess, this symbol of French science, French technology, French genius . . . and French *folie.*

What sort of a man would dare to defy the force of gravity, the wrath of artists, ridicule, ruin, and lampoon, to build his Tower in the centre of Paris? A little, bearded, barrel-chested man, with twinkling blue eyes, full of the joys of life, and an engineer *extraordinaire.* This was the man who gave us Meccano; Gustave Eiffel, erstwhile builder of bridges on the same bolt-together, step by step, principle as the Tower, fell so head over heels in love with this baroque idea that he won the competition hands down. He built the Tower, gave it his name, was now without one himself: Eiffel? Eiffel was the name of the Tower. Whatever the future might hold, he would always and only ever be the inventor of the Tower, the builder of the Tower, its begetter, but also and more especially, its prince consort. All along, Gustave Eiffel had been a man whose projects met with great success, but which would not let him be. First there was the bridge everyone said was impossible to build, over the Douro in Portugal; but he solved the construction problems with characteristic ingenuity, and built a good solid bridge while still a mere stripling of under forty. He became famous overnight, but the poor man had to build bridge after bridge

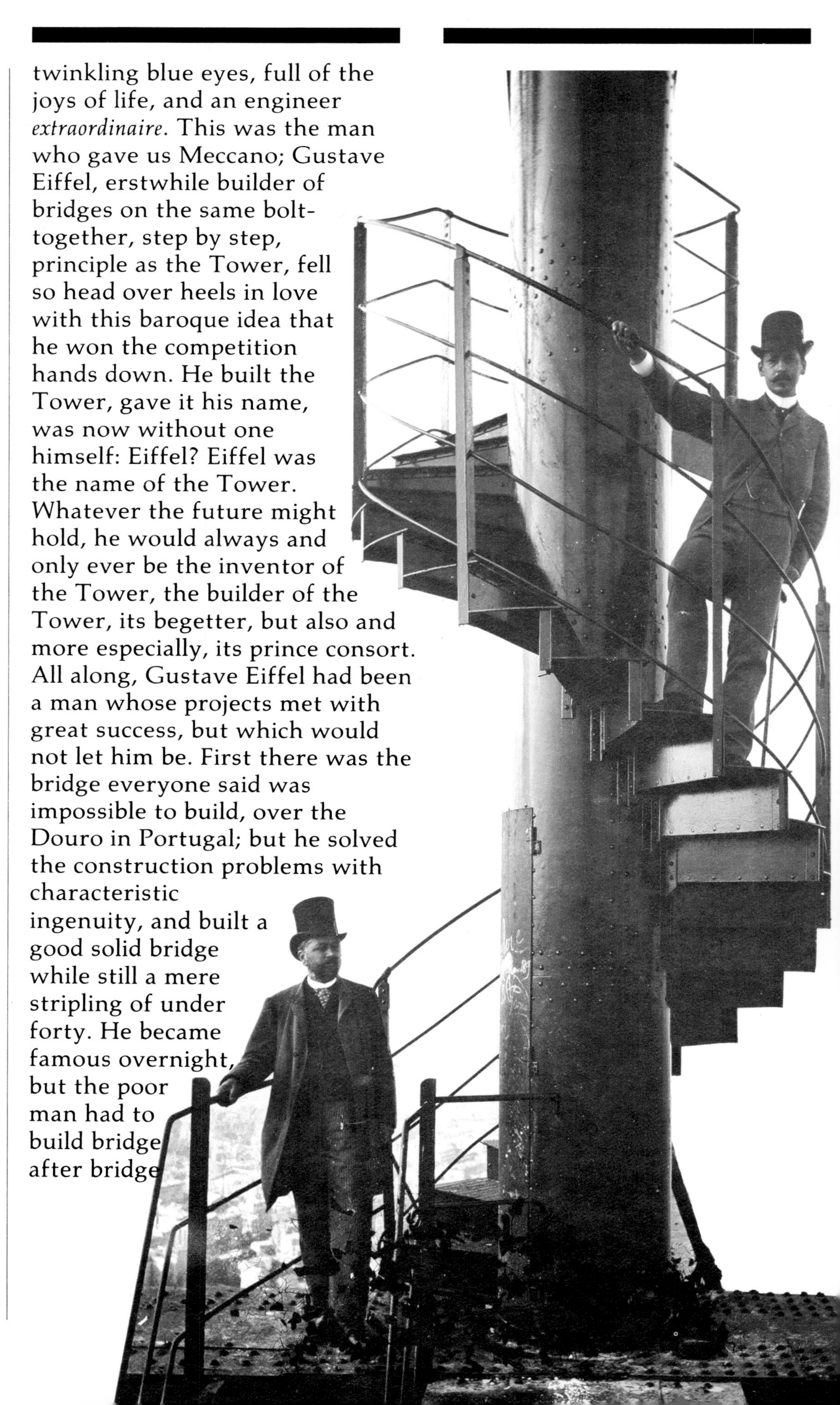

for years on end, to his great chagrin. Around the same time, planning for a predictable future, he married a woman he did not love. Only it turned out that she was quite charming and that he felt deeply for her; and when she died ten years later he was completely devastated. But right now, it was the Eiffel Tower, which he had so much wanted to build, in whose name he had taken so many risks, which brushed him aside, appropriated his name and clattered away out of reach. No sooner completed, it seemed, than Eiffel's Tower belonged to all Parisians. And yet, and yet, it had taken 5,300 drawings for Eiffel, his engineers and his architects to create their "giraffe". It had taken ten thousand pieces of iron, it had taken one hundred and fifty builders working for two years and two months, and it had taken two and a half million rivets to fix all the giraffe's bones together.

Let us add that the creature was not heavy. It weighed seven thousand three hundred tonnes, so that in a high wind its neck swayed six or seven centimetres from side to side, and that in excessive heat its head and body expanded by up to eighteen centimetres. Our "star" had a final height of 312 metres (320 with aerial). The Eiffel giraffe remained the tallest animal in the world until the Empire State Building went up in 1930. Which means that for forty-one years its gimlet eye would have swept the horizons of the Earth in vain for a rival.

Even so, to keep up to scratch, it has always needed – and always will need – 45 tonnes of fresh paint every seven years. In return for which it has been graced with four and a half million visitors over the past hundred years. It has always needed – and always will need – to be uncommonly patient, and smilingly strong, qualities maintained by an attentive and careful team, because just as no lives were lost during its construction, the Eiffel Tower has never caused the death of a visitor. In all the one hundred years no lift has come unhooked, no step has cracked, no rivet has unrivetted itself. The Tower has remained, remains, the most sensitive, most humane, most kindly giant among monuments. The desperate people who have chosen to throw themselves

There was a constant blackout, with crowds feeling their way in the darkness or in the dimmed headlights of the cars. Stripped of its illuminated advertisements, the Eiffel Tower, which Tristan Bernard called the 'Citroën widow' at the beginning of the war, was silhouetted against the bright night sky above the darkened city.

Francis Carco

from the Tower have done so against its will, in spite of its safety-rails, and in frank flouting of its character: clowning, frivolous, a trifle unbalanced, useless, or whatever people might say, the Eiffel Tower never has had, and never will have, any truck with despair. The Eiffel Tower means champagne, fluffy clouds, light headedness; the Eiffel Tower is a lighthearted, carefree, easy woman (after all, it did become female), and that is how Parisians like her.

Twenty years on, however, when his lease had expired and his costs had been covered many times over, Eiffel had to give the Tower back to the city of Paris, and he was a worried man. After all, just one civil servant grumbling about how useless it was – and lack of purpose was already becoming suspect in 1909 – might be enough to get the Tower pulled down. So Eiffel began to look for, indeed to find, a hundred and one uses for his giraffe. People had at one time fondly imagined that it might serve as an immense lamp, "by whose light Parisians in every narrow street would be able to read their evening papers as clearly as if they had been standing five metres from a lamppost." Luckily, this particular idea never got further than the concept stage. But there must be other important rôles to try? Eiffel put on his thinking cap. For a start, he declared, the air is good up there. Three hundred metres up, word went round, Parisians would feel rejuvenated, see an improvement in their complexions, feel more cheerful; and doubtless, had there been the space, Gustave Eiffel would probably have opened a clinic on the second floor. After that, he decided that it would be a receiver; certainly, this great coquette of a woman, tottering on her high heels, had as yet undreamed-of possibilities. She caught the eye, so why should she not catch the voice. Radio was making its appearance, and in the air floated nameless unquiet waves. The Eiffel Tower had only to bend her ear for the sounds to materialize. She turned to espionage, and it is said that Mata Hari was condemned to death on the evidence of the Tower's keen ears. The 1914 war was fought in the trenches, and the secret war was fought down the wires. It was then that the Tower demonstrated unsuspected shrewdness and ability. Encouraged by her creator, perhaps, this large and languid iron lady turned maid of all work. She would not be content any more simply to let thousands of curious tourists walk all over her, she would also be of service; and that is how, in 1915, a link was set up, a transatlantic intimacy between the Tower and Harlington, Virginia. Over shorter distances she enabled contact to be maintained with aircraft, with the planes which defended Paris.

After the war was over, she kept

The flying man: he threw himself from the tower and was smashed to pieces on the ground. At the autopsy it was discovered that he had died of a heart attack!

the audio-visual faith. In 1922 the first news transmissions were broadcast, and after the news came radio concerts. The first speaking newspaper went on the air in 1925, between six and seven in the evening, and, in 1934, the Tower became the first television transmitter. Having been utopian, then an object of curiosity, the Tower has become a public utility. It is not enough any more just to please, she must also serve, and alas, the second qualification will prove to be more and more indispensible for the survival of anything at all by the end of this century, or rather by the beginning of the next.

So there it will stay, there it will remain, for whatever kind of an eternity the city might envisage. Catastrophe, war or unimaginable flood notwithstanding, the Tower will stay rooted to the Champ de Mars until the day of doom. Needless to say, radio, weather forecasting, television and their respective successors improve over the years, becoming more exact, making that Tower an ever more precious asset (materially speaking, that is). But she knows that her first rôle is to impress, astound and attract, a rôle she performs to perfection. Numbers of visitors have risen constantly since 1889, and have now reached an incredible peak. Just try to imagine – wait for it! – twenty thousand people a day climbing it. It never closes, which means that every day from its four pillars to its pinnacle – wait for it! – twenty thousand people stream up; to the first stage, then up to the second if they are brave enough, and on up to the third if really courageous, there to walk in the wind, gasping in amazement, in ecstasy at the beauty of Paris. Every day that God gives. Twenty thousand people a day! And among those twenty thousand there are always a few so utterly infatuated that, every evening, they need to make the rounds three times just to check there are no fanatics concealed between the steel sinews so they can spend the night with her.

And every day, the seventy-five Tower employees, who take visitors up and down in the lifts all day long, who serve them drinks on the terraces, who sell them their tickets, who act as guides, explaining the Tower in all her mystery, all these people arrive at six o'clock in the morning and leave at six at night. They live with, on, for, because of the Eiffel Tower. Daily they offer themselves, daily they are chosen to speak in Spanish, in English, in Japanese, in Danish, in one of the myriad languages which this Tower of Babel calls for, and which echo through its stairwells and bounce off its girders. Can you imagine a whole life, a career devoted to the Eiffel Tower? Well, there have been such, for her servants are faithful, guardians from father to son, from generation to generation, maintaining her beauty and taking care of her health, as indeed they look after the needs of her never-ending stream of lovers. Their needs, and their survival, because, like any other beautiful woman, the Eiffel Tower can wreak havoc in men's lives. For a time, she was the high priestess of suicide, though falsely named. In 1964, desperate people stepped over the edge into oblivion at the rate of one a month. Jumping from the first stage means arriving at 150 kph, in one piece, and then exploding, literally, on the ground below. Jumping from the second means falling into a horrendous mincer and coming out through the girders in bits. But this only happens in a tiny minority of cases. Of the four and a half million visitors, 370 have not made it back down in one piece.

And the Tower was indeed dubbed the "Killing Tower" at one time, by people who were forgetting that the metro claims twenty times as many lives: a sinister reputation which any self-respecting giraffe must have detested. Because there have also been those who jumped but were saved by the Tower; notably a pregnant woman who, attempting to hurl herself from

For the 75th anniversary of the Tower, ten mountaineers made an ascent of the west face

The trapeze artist Rose Gold 118 metres up

the first floor, found her foot wedged between two planks in such a way that the fire brigade had to be called to get it out. She gave birth later, and with great happiness, to a dear little baby boy. And then there are people who come up to Paris from the provinces expressly to jump from the Tower. How ghastly to imagine that final journey: the train which must seem either so sluggish or so precipitate, the overcrowded station, the ominous crossing of the Ville-Lumière, the arrival at the foot of this gigantic Tower. Then the lift. Then the parapet. Then the dreadful void. Then the fall, so rapid, yet interminable; the body accelerating, time expanding. The curators are wise to this sort of suicide. Sometimes they will even follow someone during an entire afternoon's peregrination, only to see them, more often than not, come calmly down again, nonchalantly whistling, doubtless restored by the mountain air which still bathes the top two floors.

The Tower has also had its share of sporting types. The first was a Parisian baker who climbed to the first stage on stilts. In 1923, a certain Labrique came all the way down by bicycle. And recently Charles Coutard made the journey both ways by motor bike. And naturally, numerous mountaineers have climbed its 300 metres as they would scale a peak: there has even been a roped descent. There was also the more sinister experience of the tailor Reisfeldt, an early bird-man, who in 1911 put on his wings and climbed out onto the parapet (followed by his creditors, who thought they might get their money back after his successful demonstration). The poor unfortunate man trembled for three long minutes on that ledge and then jumped. He plummetted like a stone, smashed himself to bits on the ground and the autopsy revealed that he had died of a heart attack. Money makes people do really stupid things, and sanctions much cruelty! And then of course we must not forget the aviators: Santos-Dumont in 1901, who went over the top of the Tower in a balloon. Not to mention those who tried to sneak between her legs in a crude kind of test of her femininity, like the pilot Léon Collot who, in 1928, was either blinded by the sun or caught out by the telegraph

On 26th June 1940, Albert Speer shows Paris to Adolf Hitler. Four years later the Tower greets its liberators

wires which crossed his flight path, and crashed into the Tower. In 1984, the American Briarty managed this feat, but lost his licence. And last but not least, two English parachutists who jumped from the third stage in 1984 and landed without injury. All these attempts, or nearly all, have been filmed with ease because all television channels transmit from the Tower (which is perhaps the only wrong she does us!).

And finally, you may recall Edith Piaf perched on the Tower, like a sparrow indeed, in a gigantic poplar tree. Edith Piaf sang *La Marseillaise* one fine summer evening before a tearful tout-Paris. Lest we forget that partriotism is one of our giraffe's many virtues: not only did she receive and transmit coded messages during the First World War (hence her importance in the arrest of Mata Hari), but she has been a true patriot whenever her country needed her. She received that great and longed-for message in 1918: "The German government accepts the conditions of the Armistice", sending all Paris delirious with joy. Doubtless she also received the menacing message of 1940. But she also resisted the German army heroically, and incomprehensibly, in 1940, by putting all her lifts out of action at once. It is almost certain that Hitler, who wished to visit the Tower as well as the rest of the city that ominous morning, was prevented from climbing it because of his asthma. One

On the evening of the première of 'The Longest Day' Edith Piaf sings on the first level

It is said that Mata Hari would listen to the information transmitted from the tower in order to pass it on to the Germans

thousand seven hundred steps, even for the Führer, was too much. So the giraffe waited, dignified, solitary, virgin, for four years until 25 August 1944 to have her tricolour and her spirit back.

And finally, finally, the Eiffel Tower has also had its heralds. People are generally unaware that an honourable family man one day climbed to the first floor and threw his television set over the edge: "In order", as he said then, "to protest against the introduction of advertising on television." As this happened in 1968, we must assume that this particular licence-holder has not had cause to revise his opinion since then.

The affection I feel for this dear old Tower has no connection with aesthetics at all. Paris as seen from the first floor, or indeed from the third floor, is, in my opinion, far

from beautiful. The most beautiful, most human, view of Paris is from the top of something like the Arc de Triomphe; from there one can see people, and history has a human face. From such a vantage point one can see, or imagine, Napoleon's prancing generals and the massed multi-coloured ranks of their troops. To the east, the view down the Avenue des Champs Elysées to the Tuileries, a graceful motionless pavane of tree and stone: and to the west, the modern blocks of La Défense, like so many brutish self-assured dinosaurs. From not too great a height, from the Arc de Triomphe, pedestrians are still discernible and monuments still look as they ought to, the view is predictable, reassuring, more "picture postcard" altogether . . . Whereas from the Eiffel Tower, Paris is so far away, so massive and so condensed that it becomes an abstraction. And in addition to the ordinary sort of vertigo which turns my knees to jelly, repels me from the abyss and welds me to the pillar, another kind of vertigo takes possession of my senses causing the image of a strange and nameless city of the Titans to float before me, in which I can just make out, and can only identify with assistance, the Sacré Cœur, Notre Dame, the Invalides and the Panthéon. It is from planes that one sees this immense and puzzling jigsaw, never from monuments, not even from skyscrapers.

Looking from the Tower is like looking from an aircraft window

La tour Eiffel dans la brume
Joue un petit air de marteau
Elle a pris pour enclume
Le soleil dans son bateau.
Raymond Queneau.

for me. And depending on how I feel that day, I either tremble, fearful that the fragile building will crumple beneath my weight, or I console myself with the thought of all that metal between me and the all too magnetic earth. That is why the Tower's success is both fascinating and intriguing. How is it that among all the valiant hearts, all the vigorous calves, amongst all the brave and indefatigable tourists who constantly scale it, how is it that there is not each day, or even each hour, some poor unfortunate man or woman who is all of a sudden stricken with terror, whose legs give way, who clings desperately to the first attendant they catch sight of, begging him to blindfold them and lead them back down? How is it possible that tourists have so unmorbid an imagination, so unfearful an eye, how is it possible that the Tower induces such sang-froid, such gravitas, among its visitors, who must after all be so unused to mountaineering? And if I was a tourist, would I have the courage to pick my way to the top of such an unending pile of spillikins, or the courage to lean out over the preposterous void?

To tell you the truth, I'm not sure, and the daily-increasing crowd of worshippers does not cease to amaze and intrigue me: for the Tower is incredibly well-known. I must have heard at least twenty people, in my relatively restricted globe-trotting, exclaim: 'Oh! Paris! Oh! The Eiffel Tower!', as though

this were the most obvious of associations. The "Paris of the Folies Bergère" comes a poor second, the "Paris Ville Lumière" is a mere also-ran. And "Paris-Descartes" is a complete non-starter. Part of the explanation for this lies in the sheer number and variety of model Towers in existence. They sell them everywhere; people buy them everywhere. Bronze, copper, iron, and wooden Eiffel Towers; bone, porcelain, plastic and stone Eiffel Towers: soft, hard, glass and cotton Eiffel Towers. Illuminated and switched off, yellow ones, blue ones, red ones, matt ones and glossy ones. There are Eiffel Tower salt-cellars, mustard-pots, castles, lamps, shoe-horns, decorations. Eiffel Tower cup-and-ball toys. Some are made of gold, or rubber, for the most pretentious or indecent purposes one might dream up. There are millions of them in every shape and size, for every kind of use. But there is not a single one among them which is symbolic of anything at all.

Because the Eiffel Tower fires neither imagination nor memory. When all is said and done, the Tower of London brings to mind the little princes. The Great Wall of China the Revolution. The Louvre recalls the Kings of France. Notre-Dame evokes Faith. The Statue of Liberty symbolizes the severing of European chains. But the Eiffel Tower, most famous of all these, symbolizes nothing, recalls nothing, and has no message. It is called the Eiffel Tower, full stop. It was built one hundred years ago by little boys with beards to impress other little boys with beards, full stop! She has, she is, nothing but herself. But she has got something – when compared with certain sublime ancient monuments; something like whatever it is Arletty of "Hôtel du Nord" has got – when compared with, let's say, Falconetti in "La Passion de Jeanne d'Arc". Being possessed of neither beauty, nor poetry, nor class, the Eiffel Tower has sex-appeal. She is a gangling, provocative, *jolie-laide* of a woman, one without much in the way of a history, and without great expectations for the future, doubtless this creature will have had no greater purpose in life than the entertainment of her visitors. She will not have kept them for the night, or recompensed them, or worshipped them, she will have "distracted" men! She is merely free, gratuitous, and I must say that I never cease to be amazed at anything that is free. Whether it be in a city or in a person's character.

She is one hundred years old, and making allowances for her worst follies she has quite the most impudent of complexions. Ladies of this advanced age hide away, or camouflage their wrinkles, or at least cover their faces with a veil of some description: but not the Eiffel Tower. Four years ago she took advantage of the approaching centenary and had herself suddenly all lit up with the harshest, most powerful floodlights, always dangerous for a lady, albeit an iron lady. Five years ago now, not content to abandon her role as lamppost, not happy to give up providing a light for good Parisians to read their evening papers by, she decided to illuminate herself instead, exposing herself to prying eyes, with all the blemishes of the years, and in all her scrap-metal splendour. For this she has chosen, it must be said, the most beautiful setting, the most beautiful backdrop imaginable: Paris, the Paris sky, midnight blue or nearly navy in the coldest weather, or pink

3rd June 1961. Kennedy at the Palais de Chaillot

when evening mist shrouds the streetlights. Pale sky, palest blue at dawn, white stretching out towards the pink in the east. She has chosen this sumptuous setting to grace with her suddenly double-edged silhouette; because the Eiffel Tower treats herself to a little duality when she switches from her daytime to her nighttime persona.

For the look on the faces of her suitors stepping out of the lifts at six or seven o'clock in the evening, that look of joyful exhilaration, of pride in exhaustion, the look of those who have braved wind, sun or rain, the look of those who have seen the city as if from their own exalted position, not the Tower's, and who have even scrutinized the huge, docile city through the telescope, wide-eyed yet condescending, their look is not the same as that of the privileged diners descending at midnight after eating in the restaurant. They have a disquieted, knowing admiration in their eyes. It is as if the first group had stepped out of a Tintin story, or off a Meccano set, while the second has come from Belphegor and from mystery.

By night, the Tower is no longer the simple, much-fêted darling of the 1900s; she is a vamp, a *femme fatale* of high drama. She is fun by day, unsettling by night. She surprises by day, fascinates by night. By day, weather-beaten cross-struts like so many crow's feet, she is the good-time girl of the good old days; but by night she is a priestess, aloof, distant as an Egyptian goddess, one who can bring misery or joy.

In daylight she is grey, gloomy green, rust, who can tell? Whatever, a leaden metal colour, dulled by weathering, by hot sun and rain on her flanks. At night, in stark contrast, she is the blackest of jet blacks, twinkling, triumphant. So approachable in the day, a kind of advertisement, publicity announcement for tourists, she becomes a

31st May 1980. Jean-Paul II is greeted by 60,000 Poles

Mais oui, je suis une girafe
M'a raconté la tour Eiffel.
Et si ma tête est dans le ciel,
C'est pour mieux brouter les nuages.
Maurice Carême.

mysterious, almost unsettling entity at night, light years away from her origins and her history. At night, her lights ablaze, she watches over a stunned and confused Paris.

When our familiar giantess becomes our formidable mistress, exposed in her nakedness, when she is flamboyant, lit up and phosphorescent, brutally revealed by her own hand, by all the power of her spotlights, one might almost believe there to be, up there in the little cabin now empty of people, a spirit watching, keeping vigil tirelessly, casting either a sullen glare or a lively glance into the back streets, the dwelling-places, the bedrooms of the capital. It is no longer Mistinguett up there, but the goddess Kali. And one is caught out being suddenly scared that ghostly, disembodied tourists might still be drifting through the spaces, up and down the staircases, from floor to floor: the people no one has seen, who do not pay, but who have been, for ever, furtive and tormented visitors.

Yes, the Eiffel Tower becomes lyrical, mythical at night. She becomes as powerful and as eloquent for us Parisians, who are supposed to be sophisticated, as for those country folk who come from China or America, drawn to her like the wise men to the star. While unsuspecting Parisians walk beneath her feet and in her shadow day in and day out, without a second thought, at night our capital suddenly starts to respect her, perhaps even to fear her. And that is exactly how it should be, because there can be no great passion without its share of fear – and its share of smiles.

the Eiffel Tower for a poster, I decided on a trip to Paris.
As soon as I saw it, clad in its new lighting, this tower

fascinated me. Whenever I had the time, I came back to admire it.
Then began a long courtship during which, while carrying out my task, I expressed my feelings for this iron demoiselle. In the course of three years, I scoured the capital, day and night, approaching her cautiously in order to surprise her in all her poses and moods. I hauled myself up on to roofs, clambered up church-spires, stood for hours on the ends of cranes, in spite of my fear and vertigo. In this way, in all seasons and times of day, I accumulated more than two thousand photographs.
I have here collected together the most beautiful of them: a homage to the sentry of Paris, which has watched over the Parisians for a hundred years.

Winnie Denker

RESTAURANT

HOTEL NIKKO

At the entrance to the Cours-la-Reine, Simon Bolivar, hero of another continent, symbol of universality, seems to present arms to the Tower.

From both sides of the Tower, two field marshals face each other. From the Ecole Militaire Joffre (here seen from behind) can just see Foch on the Place du Trocadéro.

Musical revelry in honour of Eiffel

At the foot of the Chaillot fountains, the figures by the sculptor Leon Driver symbolize joie de vivre. *Lyre and snake . . . And what if Orpheus were to bewitch the Tower?*

Like the Chaillot palace, this group by Pierre Poisson – 'Youth' – a reminder of the 1937 Exhibition.

Paris dresse sa tour
Ainsi qu'une grande girafe inquiète,
sa tour,
qui, le soir venu,
craint les fantômes
et promène dans tous les coins les jets/
de ses projecteurs,
transformant le ciel parisien en une
épure adroitement lavée.
Pierre Mac Orlan.

Y a d'la joie la tour Eiffel part en balade
Comme une folle elle saute la Seine à pieds joints
Puis elle dit: « Tant pis pour moi si je suis malade
Je m'ennuyais toute seule dans mon coin. »

Charles Trenet.

PAVILLON BALTARD

Y a pas d'Paris sans tour Eiffel.
On la débine, on la charrie,
Pourtant partout ce n'est qu'un cri;
Paris n's'rait pas Paris sans elle,
Paris, mais c'est la tour Eiffel.
Michel Emer.

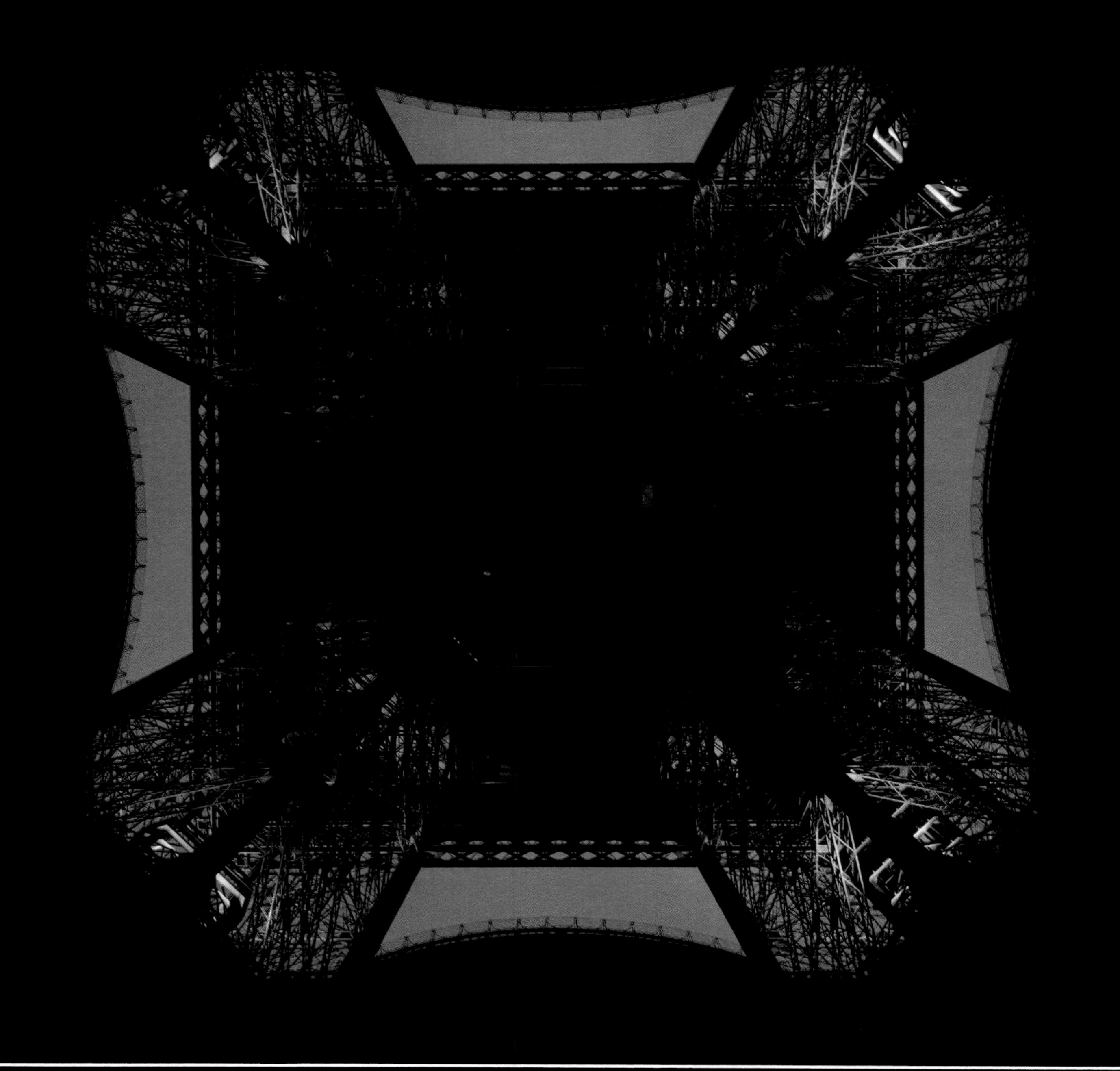

À la fin tu es las de ce monde ancien
Bergère ô tour Eiffel le troupeau des
/ponts bêle ce matin
Tu en as assez de vivre dans l'antiquité
/grecque et romaine
Ici même les automobiles ont l'air d'être
/anciennes
La religion seule est restée toute neuve
/la religion
Est restee simple comme les hangars de
/Port-Aviation.

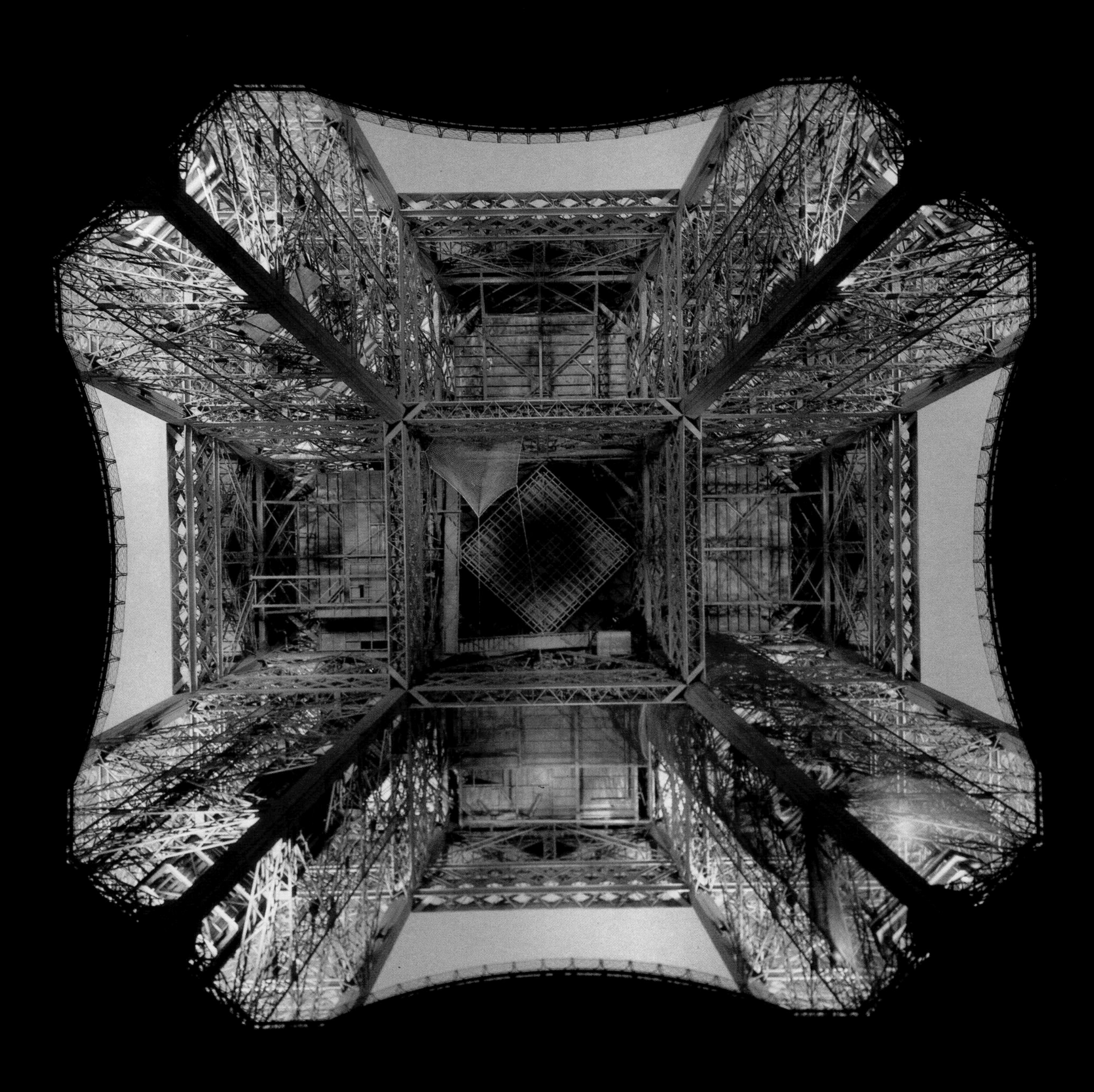

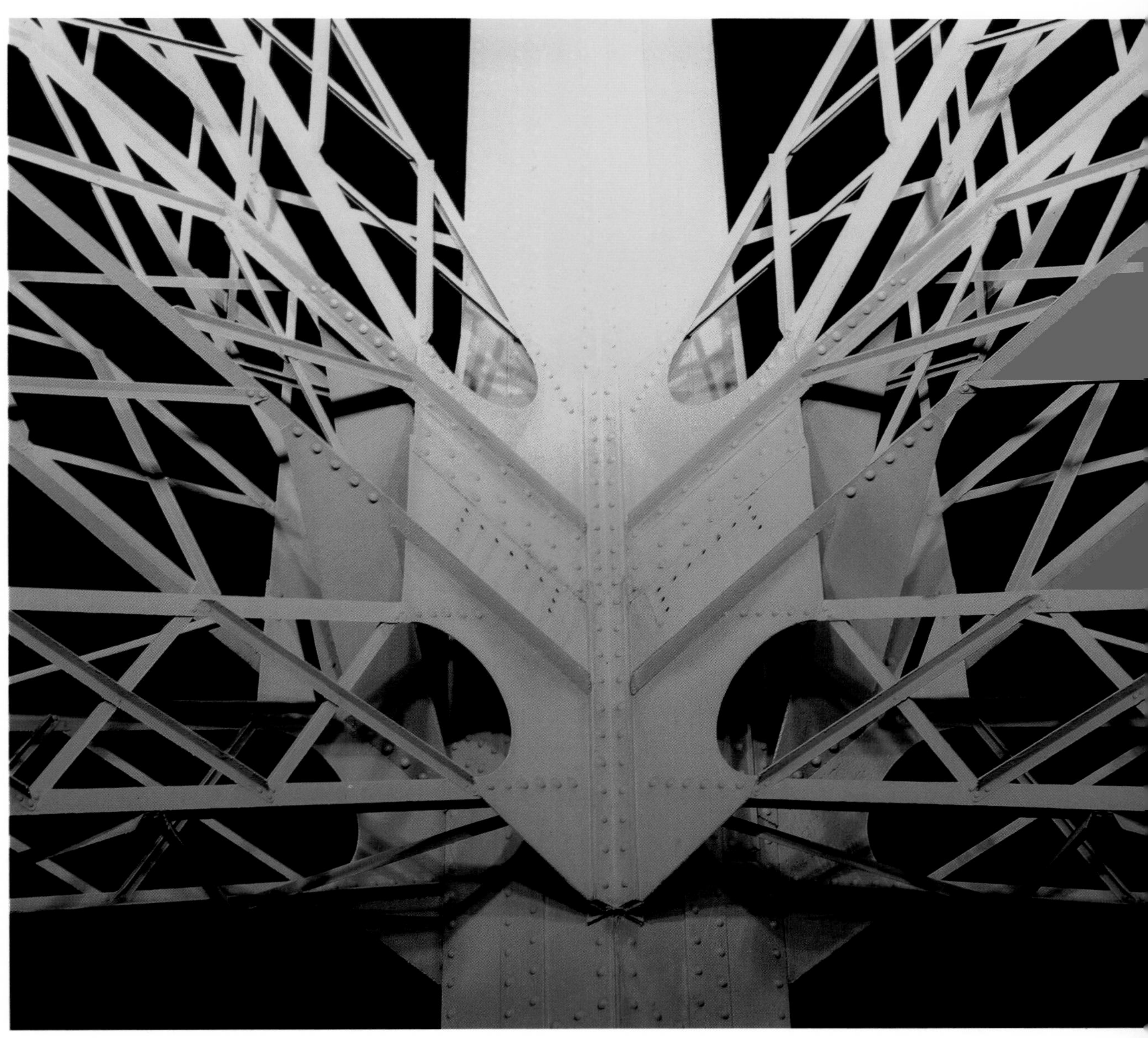

Ô tour Eiffel

....

Tu es tout
Tour
Dieu antique
Bête moderne
Spectre solaire
Sujet de mon poème
Tour
Tour du monde
Tour en mouvement.

Blaise Cendrars.

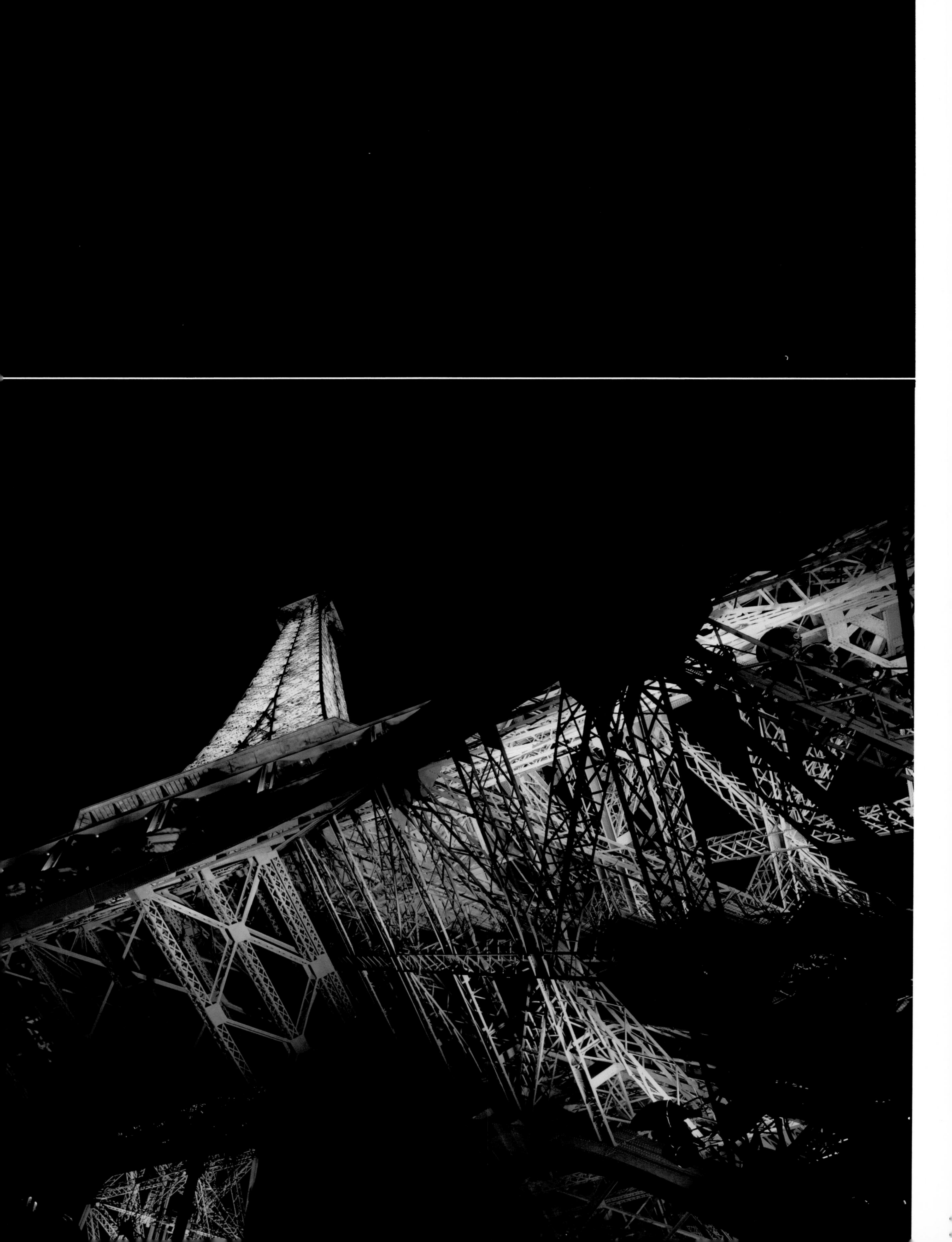

There is no journey to France which is not made, in some way, in the name of the Tower, no textbook, poster or film about France which does not put it forward as the most important symbol of a people and a place: it belongs to the universal language of travel.

Roland Barthes

Going up in the lift: the sensation is of a ship putting out to sea, but there is no feeling of sickness. Up there, far above thoughts at ground level, you become aware of grandeur, space and the sheer Babylonian immensity of Paris.

Edmond and Jules de Goncourt

On 14th July 1989 the Revolution will be two hundred years old and the tower a hundred, a coincidence which many people will want to celebrate in the restaurants on the various levels.

Just like the great flag at the heart of the Arc de Triomphe, the French colours at the top of the Tower are always an inspiration. Here they beat the air like a ship's ensign.

17.00 North east: Avenue Rapp, Avenue Bosquet, towards les Invalides and the Alexandre III bridge

12.00 North west: in the distance, the Palais de Chaillot, the Bois de Boulogne and la Défense.

06.00 South-west: the Ile des Cygnes between the bank of the Seine and the Maison de la Radio.

21.00 South east: towards Montparnasse, the Ecole Militaire and the UNESCO building.

LIST OF ILLUSTRATIONS

Page 51:
An evening walk in the park of the Champ de Mars.

Pages 52–53:
The Trocadéro fountains: a marriage of water, fire and iron

Pages 54–55:
After scaling a crane in a Louvre building site

Page 56:
On the Debilly footbridge between the Avenue New York and the Quai Branly

Page 57:
At four in the morning of 4 July 1986, a unique tribute to the centenary of the Statue of Liberty

Pages 58–59:
Windows in the Avenue de la Bourdonnais overlooking the Tower

Pages 60–61:
Avenue Rapp before lights out

Pages 62–63:
From an attic window in the Eglise St Eustache, with the dome of the Bourse opposite

Pages 64–65:
The Grand Palais lit up in blue to celebrate the Decorative Artists Fair in 1987; taken from the Quai d'Orsay. Rhapsody in Blue.'
On the right: in the bell tower of the Eglise St Eustache

Page 66:
Summer at the Tower

Page 67:
Winter at the Tower in the Trocadéro gardens at midnight

Pages 68–69:
'The Rite of Spring'

Pages 70–71:
An iron sun, a stormy night

Pages 72–73:
The lace-like quality of one of the legs

Pages 74–75:
Diamonds as big as the Tower

Page 76:
A lift to a dream

Page 77:
'*Ancient God, Modern Beast*' Blaise Cendrars

Pages 78–79:
The power and the glory

Pages 80–81:
'Between its spread legs of iron . . .' *Louis Aragon*

Pages 82–83:
The pyramids of modern times

Pages 84–85:
A spring clean every seven years

Pages 86–87:
Above left: the Tower wakes up at 9 o'clock
Above right: the fascination is immediate
Below: the pilgrims arrive

Page 88:
Midnight: the last lift

Page 89:
The wheels in the basement; a set from *Metropolis*

Pages 90–91:
In a hundred years, a great many suicides but not one accident

Pages 92–93:
La Belle France: the restaurant on the first floor

Pages 94–95:
Above: the Jules Verne, the highest and best restaurant
Below: The mirrors which adorn the stairway in La Belle France

Page 96:
The descent of the flag

Page 97:
14 July 1987

Pages 98–99:
The lighthouse of Paris, a beam cuts through the sky

Pages 100–101:
The birthday ode

Page 102:
The statue of the engineer

Pages 103–106:
North west, north east, south east, south west

Page 107:
The romance of Paris

ACKNOWLEDGEMENTS

My first thanks must obviously go to M. Bideau, who created the new lighting for the tower; he fascinated my eye and secured my objective for me. My extreme gratitude to the 'Société nouvelle pour l'exploitation de la tour Eiffel' whose team expressed its faith in me and which made my work much easier. Thanks therefore to MM. Rocher, Maresquier, Gillieron, Habert and Mme de Maneville.

I thank MM. Ody and Denis from the Societé Elitair Tour Eiffel for the faithful co-operation they always extended me.

I must also thank my friend Sheldon Cotler, from New York, who devoted his artistic talent to the creation and publication of this album.

Particular thanks to M. Francheteau, promotions and marketing director of Kodak-Pathé who provided me with film.

Thanks also to all the organizations which participated in the formulation and production of the book: the photographic laboratories Pictorial Service, Dahinden, Atelier Janjac, Sipa, Gossens and most especially Publi Mode Photo. Sotex helped with the special photographic equipment I needed.

My wholehearted gratitude to my assistants Sylvie Neveu, Francis Peyrat, Richard Rodriguez and Olivier Sprung, as well as to all the friends who helped me.

My thanks to Editions Robert Laffont; Laurent Laffont and Françoise Radux who have sustained me during these years of work.

BIBLIOGRAPHY

The Eiffel Tower, introduced by Armand Lanoux, La Difference edition.
La Tour Eiffel, Roland Barthes, chez Delpire.
La Tour Eiffel, L'Album photos de la tour raconté par Arthur Conte, Lacroix edition.

PHOTOGRAPHY CREDITS

Pages 4 and 5
Bibliothèque nationale, Paris; de Selva-Tapabor.
Pages 6 and 7
Kharbine-Tapabor; Bibliothèque nationale, Paris.
Pages 8 and 9
Bibliothèque nationale, Paris; Sirot-Ange; J.C. Charmet, (Musée Carnavalet).
Pages 10 and 11
J.C. Charmet, (Bibl. des Arts Décoratifs) et (collection particulière); Boyer-Viollet; Kharbine-Tapabor.
Pages 12 and 13
Harlingue-Viollet; Collection Viollet.
Pages 14 and 15
Bibliothèque nationale, Paris; N.D.-Viollet; de Selva-Tapabor.
Pages 16 and 17
Kharbine-Tapabor; Photo-Keystone; Sirot-Angel.
Pages 18 and 19
Photo Keystone; A.F.P.
Pages 20 and 21
Collection Viollet; Photo-Keystone; Kharbine-Tapabor.
Pages 22 and 23
Perrimond; A.F.P.

Text translated by Alison Carter

First published in Great Britain 1989 by
André Deutsch Ltd.,
105-106 Great Russell Street.,
London WC1B 3LJ

ISBN O 233 98435 6

Color separations by Reprocolor Llovet, S.A., Barcelona
Printed and bound in Spain by Cayfosa, Barcelona